My Musings

My Musings

Published by
Ruth Landis, Inc.
Chicago, Illinois
www.RuthiEnergy.com

ISBN (paperback): 978-1-0878-9272-6

Introduction

This journal is all yours. It invites you to set one appointment with yourself each week to connect with the hidden crevices of your being in a unique way. That's why, in MY MUSINGS, there are fifty-two weekly journal prompts and activities. There are a few bonus activities to play with as well, at the beginning and end of your journal, plus one at the beginning of each seasonal section.

You might ask, "Why not just do morning notes to myself daily in a regular journal?" Well, of course you can! MY MUSINGS would not interfere with that at all, only enhance your ritual, if you are already doing that. And all too easily we can get absorbed in what is arising for ourselves at the moment and write only about those things.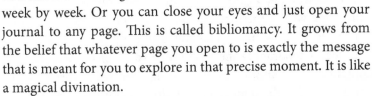

Don't get me wrong, that is extremely important. We must stay current with ourselves, so feelings don't go underground and build steam. We want to keep our emotions visible to us and encounter them as they move and transform.

However, this journal offers you additional topics that can be brought into the foreground for different ways of connecting with yourself. You can move through the book in a linear way, week by week. Or you can close your eyes and just open your journal to any page. This is called bibliomancy. It grows from the belief that whatever page you open to is exactly the message that is meant for you to explore in that precise moment. It is like a magical divination.

Do whatever intuitively suits you. Perhaps you want to draw or make art in addition to writing. That's why there are no lines on your pages; nothing is here to limit you. If you are a musician, maybe the prompt becomes the muse for a new song. The title

Introduction

MY MUSINGS means exactly that. This is completely your own. Let it meet you where you are.

And this journal is great to do in the company of others. Set aside time, in person, or virtually, with a friend or a small group. Engage in silence with one of the inspirations, photos and prompts for a given amount of time. Set an alarm. Then share your process with each other, listening as nonjudgmental witnesses only. Let that lead to a kind, safe and intimate conversation. Doing this work in a group can amplify its impact exponentially.

How was this book born?

One morning I woke up with a short inspirational phrase in my head. I recall that it was first downloaded to me at about 3 a.m., while I was sleeping. That is the "out of body" time when I generally get messages from my higher consciousness. When I am going to be giving a workshop, for instance, before going to sleep I ask for assistance from beyond. Between 2:30 and 3:30 a.m. a workshop design comes to me, just as I asked. So, on this particular morning I decided to post the revelation on social media. I felt it was a gift to share.

Then, every morning after, I would wake up with a musing or insight. This channel had inexplicably been turned on for me. Or, upon waking, a bird or animal outside my window would call to me with a message. I continued to post these and they continued to flow like a blessing. Both my husband and son had been encouraging me to compile some of my weekly blog content into yet another book. One day, Kathy L. Murphy, CEO and Founder of the International Pulpwood Queens and Timber Guys Book Clubs, suggested that I compile these particular daily morning downloads and posts into a book.

My life is very much about creating a means of accessing insights and awareness for myself and others through experiential

learning and provocative, stimulating questions. This is my joy and my calling. This is how I work with my clients and with myself. So, the concept of MY MUSINGS was born.

I have divided the book into five sections, drawn from Chinese Five Element Theory.

"Nature holds it all. It has no preference. In Chinese Five Element Theory, (the basis of acupuncture and traditional Chinese medicine) the seasons, the elements, human emotions, and every part of the body are interconnected and in a constant dance with each other. The ancient Chinese sages knew the value of recognizing this and identifying the excesses and deficiencies, the energetic balances and imbalances of the human being. They put those imbalances in context with the world she or he inhabited. Their principles embraced Nature and human nature into one whole circle of existence. That is why, to this day, acupuncture and the five elements are an intensely encompassing healing modality."
–Beyond the Bookclub: We are the Books we Must Read.

The first and last prompts in this book are each all-inclusive of the five elements. The first is called OPENING ME and the last is called ENDINGS AND BEGINNINGS. Other than these, the five different elements will have ten prompts in each, and there will also be a special prompt at the beginning of each element section as you enter the gifts of that season.

The journal prompts invite your exploration layer by layer, offering many questions. Choose to write about what feels juicy to you in the moment. Realize that you can return to any of them and write more on another day. Let each inquiry grow within you. Dive deep into yourself and fly high with the perspective of your own wise witness, as you access more and more of who you are and who you are becoming.

Now, let's begin...

Opening Me

What needs unlocking today? How have you shut tight the book of yourself and put you on a shelf? It's time to open yourself and read about what you have been avoiding.

JOURNAL PROMPT:

First, scan your body and see what feels tight or locked up. Your jaw? Your shoulders? Your pelvis? Ask the constricted places what is making them clench or lock up. Pause. Listen. See what comes. How is your body reflecting something that has happened in your life recently, a need to hunker down, avoid or hide away? Then ask your body what it needs from you to open up? What is it protecting and how can you bring safety, resources and much needed attention to yourself? At what point did you put the book that is *you* on a shelf, unnoticed and collecting dust? Write or draw about your discoveries.

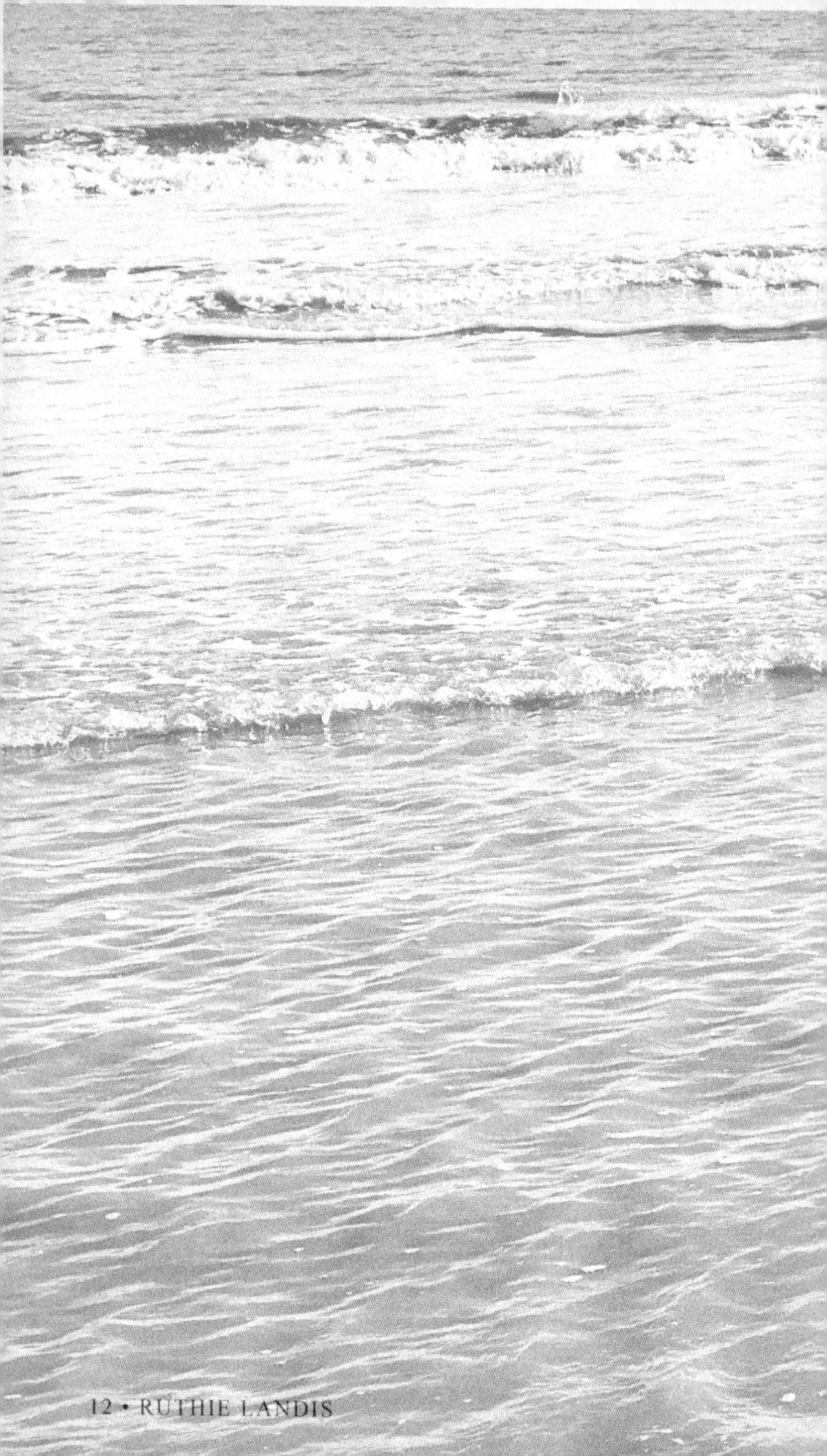

Winter
....
Water

Winter – Water

We begin with the season of Winter and the Water element. The water element is generally associated with the emotion of fear and the correlating organs are the kidneys and bladder. Those organs retain, hydrate, move, filter and release the water in our bodies. Winter is when the fertile void is present. Plants outside do not show themselves but are germinating beneath the surface, reconfiguring themselves to get ready for new life. The water element can also be associated with tears. Perhaps we cry when we are feeling afraid and un-resourced, as well as when we are sad. Fear and sadness are related and can inform each other, as we might feel quite young with both emotions.

In each of the five elements we can be in excess or in deficiency. In the water element excess is becoming waterlogged, oversaturated and preoccupied with our fears. Or we can become deficient in water, parched and desiccated in our denial of those fears. Denial often leads to hiding and secrets. There is necessary darkness in the winter, so this section has a delicious intimacy to it. Engage with it as bravely as you can. It is a time for you to go inside and be introspective with curiosity. It is a time to deeply connect with yourself and notice where you are as you travel through your life today.

On your journey, you circle familiar challenges, believing you have already tamed those internal and external dragons. You are not repeating full circle, though it may feel that way. You are in the midst of the ever-moving spiral of your life. You have changed incrementally, because as you go down to come up, you have indeed grown; you are always ascending.

JOURNAL PROMPT:

Write about some repeating challenges that continue to occur in your life. Remember those moments when you have said to yourself, "Not again!" Just because the pattern is reminiscent of other times, that doesn't mean you have not grown. After all, just noticing, with mindfulness, is a change in itself. In your exploration, take note that although the circumstances or issues feel very recognizable to you, there are many things that are different. Write about the familiarities and the significant differences of those patterns and celebrate your ascending evolution.

Winter – Water #1

INSPIRATION

On particularly challenging days, when you are afraid and feel you can't possibly go on, remember how far you have come. Take note of your track record for rising up when you are down. After all, you ARE still here. So, your success rate for getting through those hard times is 100%, and that's something to be proud of.

JOURNAL PROMPT:

Remember a time in the past when you experienced despair or felt like giving up. It was all too much. We experience this to greater or lesser degrees, whether we acknowledge it or not. Now is the moment to reflect on those times and learn something from them. Maybe you were even terrified in your anticipation of something that could happen and you felt like you couldn't face it if it did happen. What shifted? Where did help come from? How did you summon courage? How did your thoughts about the worst-case scenario prove to be an opportunity instead?

Winter - Water #2

INSPIRATION

We must make it safe for ourselves and others to be afraid. Why hide our fears from ourselves or others? In the light of awareness and acceptance, it is very interesting how quickly fear transforms itself to courage. That is, unless it isn't finished showing us what it needs to show us. Our fears have something to tell us.

JOURNAL PROMPT:

Make a completely transparent list of things you are afraid of. Read your "I am afraid of..." list out loud and notice what happens in your body when you let fear out of hiding. Acknowledging our fears can ultimately be empowering, as we find courage waiting to be claimed as well. Write about your discoveries.

BECAUSE...

We were born with an amygdala in our brains for a reason. The amygdala is a control center of your nervous system whose job it is to assess threatening possibilities and respond accordingly to protect yourself (physically or emotionally) when necessary. Fear is not bad, though modern culture often demeans it. When we don't own our fear honestly then it becomes a liability. Society has invented more acceptable terminology which we call "stressed out" or "anxious." Anxiety is repressed fear and has become pervasive in our world.

So what if you didn't suppress your fear, but rather allowed it light and visibility? What if you were grateful when you could own your fear, examine its source, and problem-solve around it? What if you didn't shut it down in yourself or in others? What if you weren't ashamed of it? What if you weren't afraid of fear? For most people just taking it out of the closet is a kind of relief and can even bring freeing tears.

Winter - Water #3

Each of us buries our secrets in the belief that doing so will keep us safe. Sometimes we push our truths down so far beneath the surface that we can't even find them anymore. Like a set of lost keys..

JOURNAL PROMPT:

Have you ever lost something at the beach in the sand? Good luck finding it. Sand is slippery and dry. Or, when the tide comes in, it gets saturated and compact. What secrets have you buried away from your childhood, adolescence, or even in recent experience? Write about this question. See if you can retrieve them, and if so ask yourself whether keeping secrets still serves you. If you can find those secrets, like lost keys, they might open you up in ways you never imagined. Close your eyes, and ask your unconscious to lead you to those keys. Once your secrets are revealed, they no longer use up precious energy as you try to hide them.

Winter - Water #4

The creative force brings movement, manifestation, some destruction, and ultimately reconstruction. She is birth and death. She digs away at the unseen. Seeing the unseen is the beginning of true transformation

JOURNAL PROMPT:

Write about a time when you cleaned the windshield of your perception and by doing so transformed something that was dying away into something new and life-affirming. Or write about something you need to let yourself see differently, from a clean and neutral place, so you can rise again.

BECAUSE...

The water element has an essential role in the creative force. In nature, water makes seeds sprout and grow, then nourishes the plants as they take root and thrive. Water fills the womb and is vital for birth. And water can create floods and hurricanes which destroy and force us to rebuild. Water can create death just as it brings new life.

Water also cleanses away the dirt from our eyes, wiping away what is foggy and unclear to us. You are forced to look at what was weak and unsupported as you reconstruct and start again.

Winter – Water #5

A tree is just a tree and knows what it is. It does not doubt itself. It does not disguise or edit itself out of fear. If only we humans could know ourselves with full acceptance of our own true natures and claim our essence, just as our tree friends do.

JOURNAL PROMPT:

Where there is unexplored fear there is doubt. When in doubt, you do not trust that you have everything you need to meet the moment, just as you are. You modify your image, avoid through deflection, or become indecisive. Write about strategies you use when you do not trust yourself. Explore the ways you deal with or navigate your self-doubt. What would it take for you to believe that you are enough for your very own unique life?

Winter - Water #6

You are changing with each breath you take and each movement you make. Your mind, body and heart are ever-changing. Holding onto your stagnant fear-based status quo takes great effort. You may cling to what you know out of fear, even as you have already begun to shift for the better. Energy leak, ya think?

JOURNAL PROMPT:

When and how do you resist change, believing that what you know is less frightening than what you don't know? Or when do you change too much, forcing change out of a fear of missing out? Write about what arises from these questions. Also explore when your relationship to change has felt very balanced, as you have intuitively followed the creative energy of opportunity with trust.

INSPIRATION

Do you want to be seen and heard or do you want to hide? Do you want to invite people into your humanity or keep that door locked? It's all a choice, really.

JOURNAL PROMPT:

Life is fleeting, fragile and unpredictable. We humans are here for a blink of an eye in the big scheme of things. Why hide yourself away in the delusion of keeping yourself safe? Show yourself. Share yourself. Write about the ways you might come out of hiding and make yourself count. You are important and so is your voice and your visibility.

Winter - Water #8

The wind whispered to me all night, "Are you running from or running towards?"

"I didn't know I was running," I said.

"You are. Something is driving you. Is it fear or is it passion? Stand quite still, listen, and find out," said the wind.

JOURNAL PROMPT:

If you run away or avoid things, you will never stop running. Those things you run from will keep on chasing you until you face them, in one form or another. Running toward your life is not a problem. Life welcomes you as you welcome it, no matter the outcome. Engagement wins the race. Write about how you discern the difference between avoidance and passion? How does running away feel different in your body than running towards?

Winter – Water #9

I tell myself and fellow change-seekers: "You do what you do until you don't do it anymore." Then one day, surprisingly, your awareness seems to move you beyond your stuck places, beyond your resistance. Did you do it yourself or was it Grace? Perhaps a collaboration?

JOURNAL PROMPT:

Write about how, one day, inexplicably, something came to you when you least expected it. Or explore how the veil lifted in a single moment, unpredictably, and you stopped seeing things one way and finally saw those same things with fresh eyes.

BECAUSE...

Sometimes you can try too hard to change. Or you can become disappointed that you have not changed enough. "Why don't I have this or that yet?" you may ask. "I am working so hard!"

It is all a matter of intention and patience. It is about accepting that you are in a collaboration with Time and the Universe. There must be an alignment. And sometimes that means you might try to let go of forcing or demanding, if you can. But even that surrender might be a change beyond your control.

Winter – Water #10

We are at the cusp. The Spring Equinox approaches momentarily with its lesson: "Perfect balance of our darkness with our light is rare. We must embrace our human imbalances as we do the inevitability of the seasons, with acceptance as well as intention."

JOURNAL PROMPT:

As you emerge from the winter and the water element, you swim upward toward the light, less concerned with your fears and your shadowy places. Just like the plants readying themselves to emerge, you too, begin to organize yourself with an attention to hopefulness and more balance. What are you looking forward to? How has the "down under" place prepared you for the visible productivity that lies ahead for you?

Spring - Wood

We now move into the season of Spring and the Wood element. The wood element is associated with the emotion of anger and the correlating organs are liver and gallbladder. Springtime is when our organizing strengths emerge. The plants are ready to push themselves up through the soil with determination and force.

Remember that each element can have its excesses or deficiencies. Sometimes, in excess, wood can become brittle and rigid, bringing forth frustration, disappointment, resentment or rage. You may feel incapable of bending, as you try to over-control. Or, in deficiency, wood can be disorganized, indecisive, cluttered and unprepared, stunted in its capacity to grow. When wood is watered and balanced, it is flexible like bamboo and goes with the flow as it builds toward manifestation. Spring is a time of hope, energy and interdependency, having reasonable expectations with committed intentionality.

Our creativity might lie dormant for a time and need to rest, as soil does, so ideas can germinate and get ready to grow. Eventually we are inspired again; we come alive, bloom and thrive, all in our own perfect timing.

JOURNAL PROMPT:

Your creativity takes many forms. It is not about making art. It is about living life artfully. Really during any season of the year you can move from productivity into dormancy or a feeling of stagnation, even if the sun is shining brightly. You can also experience great woody fertility in the middle of the darkness of winter and then flatness and depression in the springtime. We are human and our personal process does not always correlate with the external seasons. After all, we are modern humans, often out of sync with the rhythms of nature. These seasons live as metaphors to inform us about what is in balance within us and what is not. Write about some memories of dormancy in your life. Also take note of how, when in perfect timing, you shifted into inspired thriving yet again.

Spring - Wood #1

Three tree friends, dressed in their best frilly white lace flowered gowns, stand together in the splendor. I curtsy to them on my evening walk in admiration and gratitude. Spring is really here!

JOURNAL PROMPT:

Write about your relationship with springtime. How do you experience the transition between winter and spring? When you are taking a walk or even a drive, how does your body recognize the changes? How do you feel in your body as the trees start to blossom and come alive?

Spring - Wood #2

INSPIRATION

Feelings and emotions do not cause harm. Anger, sadness, and fear are only feelings that arise naturally in us as human beings. When you allow them to be expressed in a safe and creative way, they will move through you like the wind.

JOURNAL PROMPT:

Write about times when you have transformed your anger by engaging with it, not fueling it, but creatively expressing it rather than repressing it. If you have never tried this you can right now. Explore through your journaling how you might work with other emotions in a similar way. What might moving the energy of that feeling, in unexpected ways, give birth to?

BECAUSE...

Using creativity when interacting with your emotions transforms them miraculously. How does anger dance through you, if you let it? Can you drum your anger or sing it? Can you kickbox it powerfully through your body while making uninhibited sounds? Can you write about it with your nondominant hand, with crayons, from your young-person place, and then watch it burn in a safe fire outside?

After you are emptied of that angry energy, watch how its residue can be channeled into something productive, like organizing a drawer or a closet. Maybe it leads to redecorating your home or changing your hairstyle. Tap into the passion that is on the other side of that angry coin.

Spring - Wood #3

A gratitude journal is heart-warming and perspective-enhancing. A "pissed off" journal might let you feel lighter as you freely empty your triggers. Our allowed discontent can surprisingly lead us back to gratitude. Opposites attract.

JOURNAL PROMPT:

Begin now. Without shame, start writing or drawing what you are "pissed off" about. No need to edit. If this prompt doesn't feel like it applies today, set it aside for another time when you might need it. Honestly though, I find that anger (which is merely resisting what is) can be hiding and just waiting for the right trigger. Then BAM! Dig around and you might be surprised to find some angry stuff lurking in the shadows. Let yourself relish the passion behind it.

BECAUSE...

One time I created a pissed off doll and let her spout off to me (only to me) about everything that was upsetting me at the time. It was so funny and cathartic. I still have her and bring her out on occasion. She helped me move that angry energy without anyone judging me, including myself. The destination isn't to stay angry, mind you. It's just to let it out without harming anyone or turning that anger against yourself. If it is turned inward it can become depression. So start spewing.

How can you be grateful for your anger? After all, it is part of your emotional palette. And how can anger bring about intentional positive transformation when it is used kindly, wisely and mindfully? The ultimate goal is to embrace what is and bring you back to love and gratitude.

Spring - Wood #4

INSPIRATION

When Resistance arises, honor it with curiosity; don't push through it. After all, it has come to tell you there is a war going on within you. Exploring your Resistance is the first step to bringing alignment to the conflicted parts of yourself.

JOURNAL PROMPT:

Write about the times you find yourself stuck in resistance, unable to budge, and create a dialogue between the differing parts of yourself. See if you can broker a peace process between your parts so everyone is happy and the resistance can naturally dissolve.

BECAUSE...

Inside of you there is a whole community of parts of yourself. These parts have different points of view and don't always align. This is the source of your resistance.

When you have an internal argument going on that you are unaware of, you might become indecisive, out of sorts, or just procrastinate and avoid. One part of you might be saying, "I really want to do this or that." Another part of you might be feeling like, "Are you kidding me? That's going to be a disaster! I am afraid." And yet another part might be disturbed by the whole inner conflict and want to shut all parts down, playing ostrich.

Spring - Wood #5

If you don't identify the box you have already put yourself in, you can't dis-identify with it and its limiting beliefs. You set yourself free by seeing who you thought you were and instead focus on who you are ever-becoming.

JOURNAL PROMPT:

Write in the third person and introduce yourself as a neutral journalist might represent you. The journalist part of you describes who you think you are and how you believe you are perceived. This is a description of the box that others put you in as you were growing up, how others might still do that, and then how you claimed this box as your own identity. *This is just who I am,* you might think. Read what you have written. Is it all true? What doesn't feel like it matches your true essence? Are there ways you can break down the restrictions of this box? Are there ways you would like to expand who you think you are, inside and out? Write about who you can become if you want to.

Spring - Wood #6

You have sown the seeds of your soul's intention. The rain will come. The sun will shine. The wind will blow. Water, wood, fire, earth and air. Oh Life, I wait patiently to see what will grow.

JOURNAL PROMPT:

Write about what seeds you have planted in the way of intentions and dreams. Write about how you tend to these seeds of yourself each day or not. Write about seeds that have grown in your life that you did not consciously plant. Do you want to weed those out or do you want to delight in them?

Spring - Wood #7

Acknowledging your resentments aloud to yourself, instead of pushing them underground, keeps them from surfacing unconsciously. Then, you don't need to direct your resentments covertly towards those whom you resent. Resentments grow from doing things you don't want to do. You know you had a choice all along, don't you?

JOURNAL PROMPT:

Think about times you have been resentful and trace your resentment back to its source, the moment you said "yes" when you meant "no." Claiming your own responsibility in your resentment empowers you. Write about this expedition.

BECAUSE...

Resentment comes from not serving yourself first. There is nothing to resent if you knowingly make a choice that you feel is not for your own highest good. If you are about to say yes to something, you must pause and ask yourself why you are saying yes. Does this "yes" ultimately serve you?

It's one thing if someone is literally holding a gun to your head. Resent away. Save your life. Well then, saving yourself actually *was* for your highest good, wasn't it? Often you resent when you feel upset with *yourself* for betraying your own needs.

Spring - Wood #8

When your attitude feels immovable, find a part of your body to bend or roll. Let your stuckness move through you and invite your mindset to join in. Your flexible body teaches your attitude to be flexible, too.

JOURNAL PROMPT:

There are always mindsets we have that will not seem to budge. We see things in a particular way and cling to that kind of seeing. Think of an issue you cannot seem to have any flexibility around. Maybe it's something you cling to with rigidity, something you think you need to control. Find where that obstinate opinion lives in your body and move from that place. Stretch yourself and the parts surrounding that spot, holding the immovable thought as you extend and bend. Write about what happened to that attitude as you moved your body with it.

Spring - Wood #9

INSPIRATION

You see from above and at a distance the whole garden. Ahhh. You zoom in with your eyes and see just one magnolia petal. Oooh. You close your eyes and touch into yourself. Mmmm. It's all just perspective!

JOURNAL PROMPT:

Think of a situation you are facing and write as if you are a camera. First write as if seeing it from far away, neutrally and without all the specifics. Then zoom in while you write about seeing it from nearer by. Finally zoom in to a close-up and write from a very intimate and empathic place. Then zoom out again. See if you can see the forest and the trees and the ant all inclusively. How has your perception of that situation changed?

BECAUSE...

Perhaps you have heard the saying, "You can't see the forest for the trees." This expression points to the fact that you may be so preoccupied with the details you cannot see the whole picture.

Conversely, some people see only the forest and not the individual trees, or perhaps they see the ant that is crawling up the trunk of that tree. The truth is that all these points of view are important.

As you climb the mountain of your life, know that it is not straight up. You may have to grab hold of a moment that is below and over to the side from where you last had lifted yourself. That's how it goes. Still more to climb, and you also deserve to look down and see how far up you have already come.

JOURNAL PROMPT:

Write about a time where you think you took three steps forward and one step back. Write about the disappointments that arose when your expectations were not met. Write about how far you've come in spite of those disappointments.

BECAUSE...

Growth is not linear. It does not progress at a predictable speed nor does it always meet our expectations. And growth is still happening and we are still climbing. There is an anonymous quote, "The dance of transformation is a multi-dimensional and paradoxical dance in which we go down to come up and disintegrate to become whole."

Life has its ups and downs and yet you can still hold the belief that your life is moving at exactly the right pace for you, whether you like it or not.

Summer

Fire

Summer – Fire

While Spring is full of pure potential, we see how its accompanying organizational skills lead the way to the vibrant blossoms of Summertime and the Fire element. Summer can awaken your heart with emotions of joy, passion and satisfaction as the sun brings heat and intensity. Everything seems vivid in the summer.

In opposition to the benefits of the dark introspective winter, summer offers us the chance to apply the reflections we discovered in the winter and bring them fully into the light. The associated organs for summer are the heart and small intestine. Summer envelops us with vibrant colors, while the bees and butterflies pollinate in loving collaboration with the plants. Love is in the air.

But in excess, fire can scorch and burn. We can become overheated, inflamed physically and emotionally. In deficiency, we can become listless in the lazy days of summer. When we are in balance, this season offers us illumination and the capacity to energize, manifest and burst forth.

INSPIRATION

Charisma is about feeling free to shine your light brightly. In doing so you give others the invitation to shine theirs brightly as well, if they choose.

JOURNAL PROMPT:

Write about the many ways you shine your light into the world and the ways you may not. What frees you up to be radiant, sparkling and dazzling? What gives you permission to laugh heartily or sob wildly? What are the ways you dim yourself and why? Examine whether you might blame others for thwarting your animated presence. Maybe you have decided there is no room for your shine.

Also explore what deceptive messages you may be telling yourself that hold you back from claiming your lively time and space.

Summer – Fire #1

Live each day with no regrets. Stay connected with yourself and be clear. Live from your passions. When you complete your life's journey, you can feel that you have earned an honest, unapologetic bow for a well-lived life.

JOURNAL PROMPT:

Write about all the things you are passionate about. They can be anything at all. Surprise yourself. When you think you are done, keep writing more. There are passions that may have moved to the background because life can be like that. Keep your list of passions intentionally in the foreground or they will recede. Observe whether you allow yourself to do at least one thing you are passionate about every day. If not, why not? Write about days when you live from your enthusiasm and how those days feel. What kind of promises can you make to yourself to be more conscious of claiming your passions each and every day?

Summer - Fire #2

There is a difference between living your life's true purpose with humble rewards, as opposed to living from your ego's belief about what might make you happy. For the ego, it is never enough.

JOURNAL PROMPT:

Write about the gifts you have been given to share with ease and contentment. One of your purposes may be a talent to bring laughter, as an example. There may be more than you consciously know. Distinguish them from "should," obsessive goal setting, and proving through achievements. That is where the disconnection occurs, between true purpose and the ego's external, insatiable desires.

BECAUSE...

Having desires is built into the human structure. You are hungry for this or that, in your body, your heart and your mind. That's what activates you to feed yourself on all levels. This is life sustaining. And we know we can starve ourselves or overeat, when we are out of balance in our physical desires. Living your life's true purpose is not an appetite to run from. It nourishes you and those around you. It is your calling and it is never desperate, because it flows organically from your essence and the special gifts you innately have.

In fact, engaging with your purpose (and you may have many) is satisfying just in the doing of that which you are naturally compelled to do, for the highest good. It is only when your ego intervenes and loses sight of what you are really here for, becoming ever-demanding, that you move into excess or deficiency. At these times you can burn yourself out obsessing to please and strive, or else collapse in disappointment over results that displease you.

Summer – Fire #3

You can only speak your truth to the degree that you allow yourself to see it. The whole of it, dark and light. In this way, you stop hiding from yourself and your unconscious edits. Since speaking expansive truth sets us free, it's time to pull up the blinds.

JOURNAL PROMPT:

Write about your voice. How do you express yourself truthfully? When you have something important to say, to whom do you say it and when? Or do you keep it to yourself? Do you communicate operating from assumptions about how you might be heard? Do you speak while trying to manipulate the situation? Do you get clear with your feelings and the whole picture before you speak? How do you prepare yourself for communicating with others from an empowered and inclusive place? If this is hard for you, in general or with certain people, what can you do to improve your skills in this area? We begin by recognizing. Since the body never lies, what data is it giving you as you dive deeper into these inquiries? As you write, pay attention to your mouth and neck area. Do you cough or clear your throat? Does your throat feel constricted? Is your mouth dry? Journal about all the questions, being as bravely transparent with yourself as you can be. Your pure and honest voice matters. Get to know it better.

Summer – Fire #4

INSPIRATION

This morning three squirrels played and leapt with delight, squeaking their version of laughter. "Lighten up! Life is fleeting. Have fun today!" they giggled. A crow landed and cawed in agreement. If only you could share in their simple joy.

JOURNAL PROMPT:

How often do you allow yourself to really play? Squirrels can be very productive around their survival when they need to be but they play hard with such glee. Watch some squirrels for a few minutes. Imagine yourself carving out time for playfulness, just for the fun of it. Imagine being intentional about your attitude at times, steering it from serious to entertaining and giddy. Write about times when you have done just that. How might the quality of your life be enhanced if you did this more often?

Summer - Fire #5

You put your hand on your pounding heart:

"What's wrong?" you ask.

Your heart says, "Today I feel lonely."

You reply, "Okay. I am here with you. What do you need from me?"

Your heart replies, "You."

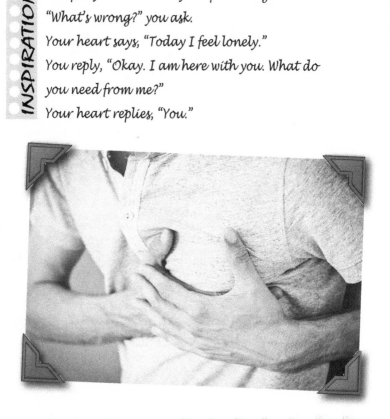

JOURNAL PROMPT:

Write about how you may disconnect from one of your centers of intelligence (head, heart and gut) more than you do the others. Who leads most of the time? How might you create equality between all three centers and embody an integrated team?

BECAUSE...

We have three centers of intelligence, at least, not counting our noetic sense - deep knowing without actual knowledge - what some may call intuition. Your head/thoughts, your heart/feelings and your body/gut all contribute to your whole integrated self.

True presence with yourself and others requires an alignment between those centers. If one center dominates you have abandoned your others. If you over-think you may lose touch with your heart and body-knowing. If you are only engaged with your body, you may be disconnected with your heart and head. The heart is often given the least respect and acknowledgment because we live in a world that finds heart-knowing frivolous or "emotional."

Summer – Fire #6

Grandma Magnolia opened her waxy, sweet, fragrant flowers yet again in the summer. Twice bloomed. With scarred bark, so many limbs lost and new ones grown, Maggie keeps on reaching for life until her time comes. She just keeps on blooming. So can you!

JOURNAL PROMPT:

Magnolias are believed to be one of the most ancient flowering trees, with fossils discovered dating back to sixty million years ago. So they are wise and effective in their evolution. Most years this particular magnolia tree blooms twice, in the spring and the summer. Sometimes life delivers challenges, and forces you to recreate yourself. These are actually wonderful opportunities to re-envision yourself and bloom anew. Write about times where you hit a dead end and found you had to reinvent yourself. How did you manage to find ways to bloom again?

Summer – Fire #7

Today you woke up and shame greeted you. This time you embrace the unacceptable in yourself. You love the unlovable, and all at once you feel whole again.

JOURNAL PROMPT:

What makes you feel ashamed? Are you aware that you sometimes feel shamed by others? If you are, how do you behave? This little guy covers his face. Some people blush. Still others retreat or some attack when they are embarrassed, mortified, or humiliated. There are those that deflect or blame. Meet your own shame with compassion as you write about how it shows up for you in your life. Can some sensations in your body help you recognize when shame appears? Emracing your shame is another opportunity to make yourself a better friend to yourself and others.

Summer – Fire #8

Moments of recognition, when your blind spots are exposed to you, can be so warm and tender if you let them be. You can come to these exposing revelations with gentle generosity and a full-out loving belly laugh. After all, you are beautifully human.

JOURNAL PROMPT:

Journal about times when you have been harsh with yourself as a blind spot has been uncovered. Also write about times when you could approach the unveiling lightly and with gentle laughter, accepting your humanness.

BECAUSE...

What if you could laugh, or smack your forehead with a "whoops," when you have been exposed? What if you could sincerely apologize for a mistake that you were caught doing, while still being kind to yourself?

The summer light has illuminated that which has not been seen before. Thank you Sun for the revelation. If you knew better, you'd do better.

Summer - Fire #9

INSPIRATION

Forgiveness is not easy. You can't snap your fingers and forgive because you think you should. Often, forgiveness comes as a moment of grace. One morning you may wake up and the bitterness is gone. What a gift! The prize of authentic forgiveness is freedom and a clean, wide-open, loving heart. It is precious and comes in an organic and timely way.

JOURNAL PROMPT:

You can engage in the process of forgiveness with intention but not force, kindly accepting that it is a process. Write about your relationship with forgiveness.

BECAUSE...

It has been said that not forgiving weighs on the person who cannot forgive. At the same time there is no magic button to push to make forgiveness happen. And would you want it to be so easy? Perhaps you are attached to the weight of it and you feel it somehow serves you to not forgive yet. That is understandable. Perhaps it is worth the weight as you may perceive it as protection. Perhaps it is an important part of your story for now. Until it isn't.

The pressure to forgive before you are ready can lead to you judge yourself, and then you can add forgiving yourself to the pile. Authentic forgiveness unpeels itself in layers. Contrived forgiveness usually resurfaces with moments of pain and resentment when you least expect it.

*You wake up **new** again. Who will you be today? Your heart is beating. Your lungs take a big breath. Your heart encourages your mind, "Please still yourself, dear one, and let yesterday's demands go, so you may greet your newness today, wide open with pure potential."*

JOURNAL PROMPT:

Try the ritual at right and write about what you discover. Journal about how you may drag one day into another without being aware of it. Or journal about how you may forget your day too quickly without acknowledging the growth.

BECAUSE...

A ritual I learned about years ago is to fill a bowl each morning with water to represent the intentional filling of your day ahead. At night you take the bowl and empty it as you water your plants or you just give the water back to the earth with gratitude as you reflect on the gifts of the past day. Those gifts have come in all their forms, both as challenges and successes.

Then you turn the emptied bowl upside down as you go to sleep for the night and enter your resting dream life. You leave mistakes behind and offer them back to Mother Earth, taking only the teachings with you. Sometimes you will even process what you learned through your dreams. And when you wake up, you begin again, filling the bowl with water for this new day.

Harvest Time

· ·

Earth

Harvest Time - Earth

After Summer there is a brief period, what we might call harvest time. This is the Earth element. The associated emotions are rumination, worry, pensiveness, as well as contentment, satisfaction and safety.

As we harvest all that we have sown in the previous seasons, we contemplate how well we have nourished ourselves emotionally and physically. We also take note of which seeds took hold and flourished and which did not.

The organs associated with harvest time are the stomach and spleen. In excess, have we over-given? In deficiency, have we not given enough to ourselves and others? How is our self-care? In balance one thinks of Mother Earth, our great provider and all she offers us abundantly, inviting gratitude and pure generosity to ourselves and others.

And Grandmother Moon sings to me, as she reveals herself in her various forms. "Do as I do, my dear one, and shine whether you feel whole or not. I am always whole, as are you, whether I appear that way or not."

JOURNAL PROMPT:

The moon appears in all shapes throughout her monthly cycle. She is never less than whole. She appears to you differently based on her angle and how the sun reflects her back to you from her surface.

Use this metaphor as you write about your own wholeness. Write about how you may feel less than whole sometimes and why. Wholeness is all inclusive.

Harvest Time – Earth #1

INSPIRATION

We are just a screen. Approval from another is all about them. Disapproval from another is all about them. You are merely their projection. And here you thought it was all about you.

JOURNAL PROMPT:

Write about how you distinguish between what is really about you and what is projected upon you by others. How do other people's projections onto you distort your own accurate assessment of yourself? Also write about how you may project your stuff onto others. When do you do that, about what themes, and onto whom? We project what we want to disown.

Harvest Time - Earth #2

INSPIRATION

Pain is fertilizer. It helps you grow. It is sprinkled by the Universe onto your little personal garden plot to enrich the soil of your existence. Nourish yourself with kindness in the midst of your pain.

JOURNAL PROMPT:

How do you nourish yourself when you are in pain? How can you be gentle with yourself even as you uncomfortably grow from your pain? How can pain accelerate your personal growth? Write about painful times in your past, either physical or emotional, and how, in retrospect, you grew from those times.

Harvest Time - Earth #3

You are receiving in each moment, though you may not recognize this. You receive the air you breathe and the sunlight you absorb. Great Mother Earth holds you and sustains you. You have much to be grateful for.

JOURNAL PROMPT:

What is your relationship with receiving? Do you access receiving easily? For some, receiving feels vulnerable. Are you a gracious receiver or not? Are you disappointed in what you receive? If so, why do you think that is? And what is your relationship with gratitude after receiving? Is it natural for you to feel grateful? How do you express gratitude? Where do you feel it in your body?

Harvest Time - Earth #4

Meditate on your predisposition to overuse or underuse saying yes, no, or maybe. What is your default? What is your habitual knee-jerk response? You must pause, check in, and align head, heart and gut in your conscious decision-making.

JOURNAL PROMPT:

How do you make decisions? Do you tend to say yes automatically? Or do you habitually say no, without really giving it much thought, as a protective mechanism? Do you avoid commitment by saying maybe a lot? Is "maybe" a part of your vocabulary? Write about your relationship to these three words and what it reveals about you on a motivational level. Also explore what it feels like when your head, heart and gut are not in alignment when you are trying to make a decision. Reflect on decisions you have made impulsively and came to regret later. What might you have done differently?

Harvest Time - Earth #5

How do you measure your life? What do you honestly believe you deserve? What criteria do you use to weigh your worth? What is the spreadsheet you refer to in determining whether you are living a life that matters?

JOURNAL PROMPT:
The inspiration is already a journal prompt. Write about those questions and, in addition, create a list of values that are near and dear to you. Where did those values come from?

Harvest Time - Earth #6

What if you could let yourself be mediocre today? What if you could let yourself be "good enough?" What if you could be okay with coming in last? After all, someone has to. How much stress might melt away if you could give yourself permission to embrace your "ordinary?"

JOURNAL PROMPT:

What is your relationship to the word ordinary? Write about what it's like to have an ordinary day. What does that mean to you and how do you feel about it? Now explore what it feels like if *you* feel ordinary. Could that ever be okay? Or even a relief? Or does it feel unacceptable? How has your relationship to the ordinary been shaped by the world you live in?

Harvest Time - Earth #7

Plant seeds of your heart's desire each day. Tend to them with care, paying attention. You have no idea what will grow. Still, you must keep planting. And then be in awe and gratitude for what does take hold.

JOURNAL PROMPT:

Reflect back on seeds you planted earlier in your life, your dreams and wishes. Perhaps they are your "if onlys." Have you stayed connected to those dreams or set them aside? Have you tended to them and prioritized them? If you have let them go, why? Do you feel good about those choices? What are the dreams you committed to which did not take hold or manifest? Yet. Did you experience grief around the ones that got away? Are there new seeds waiting to be planted and, if so, what are they?

Harvest Time - Earth #7

Is rest a waste of time? "The clock is ticking. Much to do!" says your mind, guilt-tripping you. Maybe your body and spirit are tired today. The wise kitties and puppies know. What sweeter and more loving gift than a simple nap?

JOURNAL PROMPT:

The Earth element is about nourishing yourself and self-care. Are you excessive or deficient in this? This is the time of harvesting and replenishing yourself. You deserve rest as you have moved through all the seasonal cycles that have come before this moment. You deserve the right to partake in your own bounty. Write about your self-care practices. Are there any ways to enhance them?

Harvest Time - Earth #9

INSPIRATION

Nothing like sleeping with the window open as the gentle rain sings, softening your restless thoughts. Nothing like waking up sure that the rain has cleared some hopelessness and worry away, the wet earth absorbing it. A new day.

JOURNAL PROMPT:

You may run the same thoughts over and over in your mind, without relief. Rumination is a part of the Earth element when it is out of balance. How do you free yourself around your worries, whether regarding past choices or future ones? How do you find ways to cut yourself some slack, perhaps lowering the unreasonable expectations you have placed on yourself? Denial isn't the answer either, because it is a form of repression that often feeds rumination. How do you move from worry to safety and contentment? Write about your process around bringing your earth element back into balance.

Harvest Time - Earth #10

The orange and gold fishies in the little city pond
emerge in the morning from the cool, leafy bottom.
Mouths open like baby birds as they swarm toward you
on the water's surface. "I'm hungry for life! Feed me!"

JOURNAL PROMPT:

How are you hungry for life? What feeds you? When do you feel satisfied and how do you know you are? How does your body tell you that you are full, literally and metaphorically?

Autumn

· ·

Metal/Air

Autumn - Metal/Air

Finally, we reach the last season, Autumn, when leaves must let go of their place on the branches to make room for new growth. All the feelings connected to bursting life must reach the end of this particular cycle. The orange and gold colors of the leaves eventually change to brown; they dry up and shrivel, floating to the ground, blanketing it, as we begin again. This is associated with the element called Metal/Air and the lungs and large intestine. We breathe in the oxygen we need. We breathe out all that we don't need. Our bodies process the foods we eat, digest, and hold onto what is useful. Our large intestines eliminate and let go of what does not serve our bodies.

In life, it is sometimes sad and difficult to let go and leap full out into the unknown prospect of change. That's why the emotion of grief from letting go is associated with autumn. A grey heaviness may set in as we move back into introspection. Yet touching into loss and perhaps embracing our emptiness may bring a different kind of hopefulness, trust and courage. We move toward the year's end with the knowledge that renewal is on its way.

Life is a series of losses and findings, of feeling lost and feeling found. Just as you despair, something new arrives to nourish you, if you stay open and pay attention.

JOURNAL PROMPT:

Write about times you feel you have lost yourself and then found yourself again. What happened that created the disassociation, disconnection or dis-engagement with yourself in the first place? Write about how you found your way back to yourself again.

Autumn - Metal/Air #1

INSPIRATION

And the sky said to you, "I am grey today to remind you that everything is not always one way or the other. Sometimes living in the grey of things is exactly what you need."

JOURNAL PROMPT:

How does grey actually feel in your body? Try not to assume it feels one way or another. Let your body tell you. Write about what your body says to you. Journal about things that are greyish and out of focus for you right now. What kind of opportunities does grey offer you?

BECAUSE...

There are autumn days that bring us grey. What a gift. Life is not just the dichotomy between black and white. Things can't always be crystal clear. Cloudy and foggy aren't a dismal weather forecast; they're a beautiful part of life.

Grey allows you to hang out in the "I don't know" place for a while. It invites you to discover the nuance of a situation and the in-between space.

INSPIRATION

A hawk appeared in the little city backyard, big and bold, and perched on a tall fir tree. What message do you bring, powerful hawk? "Pull your vision up and change your perception of things to a higher perspective or you will never see the whole picture."

JOURNAL PROMPT:

Choose a certain stance you've taken on a situation or an opinion you have. Write about what it would be like to let go and "re-see" from different points of view. This invites you to see with fresh eyes.

BECAUSE...

The hawk brings the medicine of clarity. She has the capacity to see details from a distance and she can also see an expansive view from afar.

Sometimes, when you are absorbed in an attitudinal posture that you sense needs freeing up, and you can't seem to let go of the way you are seeing things, imagine you are your friend the hawk, able to fly from branch to branch, seeing the same thing from different viewpoints.

Autumn - Metal/Air #3

Being CHOSEN feels terrific. When you are NOT CHOSEN, it is a blessing. Each experience gives you an opportunity to evaluate yourself honestly, with love and compassion.

JOURNAL PROMPT:

Reflect on times when you have been desired or chosen. What did it feel like? What happened in your body? Try to re-experience that sensation. What were your thoughts associated with being the chosen one? Recognize whether you truly felt empowered, or if, perhaps, you gave a little of your power away to the chooser. Explore the consequences of that.

Also think about times you were not desired or chosen. What was that like? Notice how you might have given your power away then too, or not. Write about these two opposite reactions. How do you hold onto your self-empowerment, regardless of external feedback?

Autumn - Metal/Air #4

INSPIRATION

If only you could allow yourself to be vulnerable, to bring all your hidden parts, and your blind spots, out into the light with acceptance. Then, your vulnerability would lead you to genuine empowerment and illuminated strength.

JOURNAL PROMPT:

How does a tree feel when it has lost all its leaves? Do you imagine it feels less like a tree? Does it even ponder its bareness? When you hide away parts of yourself because you are afraid of how you might be perceived, you run the risk of losing your true strength. Strength comes from embracing your wholeness, even as things fall away. Write about your relationship with vulnerability in yourself or in others. See where this exploration leads you.

Autumn - Metal/Air #5

If you hold a person who has hurt and disappointed you to your own standard of what is right and good, you will continue to be hurt and disappointed. You must understand and accept the other person's true capacity. Why knock at a cupboard door seeking nourishment when the cupboard is empty?

JOURNAL PROMPT:

Remember times when you have been disappointed by another person and feel that they have let you down. Is it possible your expectations of them were unreasonable? Perhaps you didn't see them as they really were, but rather how you wanted them to be. How have your disappointments been related to you seeing people through dirty and distorted glasses?

Autumn - Metal/Air #6

INSPIRATION

You hear the airplanes overhead; you see them cut through the blue sky and the clouds. You hear the birds in chorus and watch them flutter their wings in the sky. You hear the geese honking as they fly with their tribe in formation, free yet connected. We all want to soar in our own way, don't we?

JOURNAL PROMPT:

How would you define soaring for yourself? Have you ever felt like you soared? Anything that flies optimizes its use of the wind beneath its wings. The air element is beckoning us to use its invisible support. Where is your air and how do you use it?

Autumn - Metal/Air #7

Humility is not self-deprecation, it is an accurate assessment of your true value and contributions. Humility is seeing yourself with balanced eyes.

JOURNAL PROMPT:

If you could assess yourself without preference of what is good or bad, better or worse, how would you describe yourself? For instance, by humbly saying, "I have a gift for figuring out puzzles." Or, "I generally am tuned into other people." Or, "I make colorful and textured art which seems to evoke feelings of peace in others." Or, "I am an intuitive and skillful chef." These are all a balanced view of you and your innate gifts. Write about yourself with balance and appreciation.

Autumn – Metal/Air #8

How do you enslave yourself? With unproven, perhaps false, habitual and conditioned thoughts and beliefs? Look through the bars of your self-made prison. What's on the other side? The key to your freedom is to let yourself find out. How about now?

JOURNAL PROMPT:

Limiting beliefs about who you think you are or have to be confine you. Although you may not realize it, you hold the keys to unlock those constraining thoughts. You must first recognize them through awareness. Then question or challenge them. Are they true? These are your keys. Write about yourself and what holds you back from being your free, ever-unfolding and expansive self.

Autumn – Metal/Air #9

INSPIRATION

Self-deception is not lying, exactly. Lying is conscious and intentional. Yet, self-deception often bites you back the same way a lie can. How do you deceive yourself and why?

JOURNAL PROMPT:

We say things to ourselves and others automatically rather than carefully examining what we're really experiencing before we speak. For example: Is it really true that I'm feeling fine? Do I honestly believe what I am saying? Write about ways you self-deceive and why you default to them.

BECAUSE...

Phrases that reek of self-deception like these might be familiar to you. "I'm fine, really." "I have things under control." "No, I'm not angry." "I don't need any help. I can do it all myself." "I'm not hurt. It's all their problem." "There's nothing wrong." "I've got plenty of time to get it all done." "I will do it later. Really, I will. I just don't have time now." "It's okay. They just don't want me around. I understand." "It's good enough. I don't care."

In Hamlet, Shakespeare has Queen Gertrude respond to what she perceives as an insincere reaction by saying, "The lady doth protest too much, methinks." This has become a common expression that we use to call out what we perceive as denial, defensiveness or self-deception in another.

INSPIRATION

Creativity can be capricious, fleeting, and sometimes hard to tame. She arrives unexpectedly, a windstorm. You must wait patiently for her next visit like a faithful lover.

JOURNAL PROMPT:

You may have times in your life when you feel flat and unproductive. You may despair that this is a permanent state that will never change. Perhaps you feel restless and unsettled or stagnant. You may feel that life is passing you by. And just as it may be raining and dismal one moment, the sun can come out from behind the clouds again in the next. Faith is required when you feel this way.

Remember that forcing productivity will result in contrived and inauthentic results. You must have the confidence and conviction that life is cyclical, and that the wild and satisfying creative force within you will rise again. Patience, at these times, is love. Write about how you navigate these in-between times.

Endings Become Beginnings

"Stay with me," you say to yourself. "Sometimes you leave me. I don't know where you are going." Your inner dialog continues and you're really listening now: "I am the container of your soul. I am your connection to the deepest parts of yourself waiting to be known and felt, and to the rest of all that is." You respond by saying that if you do float away, you promise to return.

JOURNAL PROMPT:

As you come to the end of this journal, consider how can you create a new beginning. What vows can you make to yourself so that you stay in close touch with *you* and don't float away? Check in with yourself to know whether you have unconsciously put the book of yourself on a dusty shelf, out of reach. How has the journey with this journal allowed you to become your own best friend?

In Gratitude

I begin by thanking The Great Unknown for dropping these inspirations into my consciousness each morning. I have adapted them to speak directly to you, the possessor and creator of your journal. *My Musings* are in fact *Your Musings*. This book is dedicated to YOU. As you have reflected and journaled, I hope you learn to love yourself more and better. These inspirations originally came as messages spoken directly to me, and now I share them with you. We are all mirrors for each other, are we not?

I, once again, offer the sincerest gratitude for the all-encompassing and limitless Shari Stauch, who has guided me through this unfamiliar new terrain as author. With each of my books she offers insights and direction, and helps my books find their readers. With *My Musings*, Shari envisioned all the aesthetics of the journal and made it come alive on the page, inviting you, the reader, to fill the journal with yourself. Shari, I continue to stretch myself with you as my Sherpa.

I want to thank my assistant, Molly Hostetter, who is so patient with me and supports me creatively and technologically, from collaborating in the editing of my videos to proofreading my books, to keeping me organized and on task in the marketing department. You have been a godsend.

I am so grateful for my friend, Kathleen Barber, a brilliant acupuncturist, who has been as passionate about the Five Elements as I am, since the day we met. Kathleen helped me sort the inspirations into the elements, which is not an easy task and always food for thought.

Thank you, Kathy L. Murphy, for inviting me into your community of great authors and folks passionate about reading and writing. You told me these inspirations should be a book, and now they are. And *My Musings* invites everyone to create their very own book.

Thank you Annalee Letchinger, for your precise and careful proofreading.

Finally, I thank my husband, Ed Letchinger, who builds me up when I lose faith, reads my writing to me aloud, improves my clunky sentences and checks every single comma. *I love you.*

Ruthie Landis

Ruthie Landis believes life is an opportunity to learn and grow. She is a best-selling author of **Beyond the Bookclub: We are the Books We Must Read**, **Acting Lessons for Living** and its accompanying **Guided Journal**.

Her other professional roles include facilitating growth as a body-centered psychotherapist and coach, certified hypnotherapist, Enneagram teacher, award-winning international workshop designer, trainer, and facilitator. She is a visual artist, actress, director, acting and presence development coach, Spiritual guide, and Reiki master.

In addition to using theatrical and psychotherapeutic tools, Ruthie uses Nature, Ritual and Ceremony, life transition directed interior design, and the Chinese Five Element theory.

It is her mission to find ways to reclaim our wholeness with gentle, insight-driven change. Her intention is to bring all these interests and skills together to co-create unique encounters of waking up, self-empowerment, and healing.

For more info visit ruthienergy.com and Ruthie Landis YouTube.